Oslo Travel Guide

The Top 10 Highlights in Oslo

Table of Contents

Introduction 6

1. Holmenkollbakken & Skimuseet 9

2. Vikingskipshuset 12

3. Norsk Folkemuseum 15

4. Den Norske Opera & Ballet 17

5. Akershus Slott & Festning 21

6. Frognerparken 25

7. Nasjonalgalleriet 29

8. Det Kongelige Slott & Slottsparken 31

9. Oslofjord 33

10. Munchmuseet 35

Introduction

Founded over 1000 years ago, Oslo began as a strategic trading location and has over the centuries continued to serve as a hub of activity for Norwegian trade. The capital of Norway has a rich history as a coastal city and boasts numerous historical and cultural sites with enough activities to please the modern traveler venturing into this thriving metropolis.

Depending on the season, Oslo changes dramatically from green fields on long summer days to a snowy wonderland of winter. The only constant is that there is always something to enjoy and discover in the Norwegian capital. No matter the season, you are bound to enjoy this great city and its sights.

For such a small capital by most measures, Oslo has a surprisingly large collection of interesting museums, including those found on Bygdoy Peninsula. The most popular is Vikingskipshuset where you can enjoy great Viking ship discoveries, in addition to other archeological finds from the Viking tombs uncovered around Oslofjord.

Akershus Fortress dates back to the year 1299 and has always held a lot of importance to Oslo due to its strategic location. The medieval castle and royal residence features a number of magnificent halls, banquet halls and government reception rooms. Also of interest are the Royal Sarcophagi buried in the small church at the Castle.

Don't miss out on the Holmenkollbakken, one of the most famous ski jump arenas in the world. Rising 60 meters above ground, this is the site of one of the world's oldest ski jumps. Enjoy the thrilling ride of the jump or watch competitors toughen it out at the arena. At its museum, the Skimuseet, you will find plenty of information relating to the history of skiing.

Frognerparken is home to the Vigeland Sculpture Park, an innovative park designed and built by Norwegian artist, Gustav Vigeland to exhibit his famous sculptures. The interplay between the sculptures, the architecture and the green areas of the park makes for a breathtaking sight.

The islands of Oslofjord are another must see when visiting Oslo. The islands, each with its own interesting history, are famous for hosting attractions such as beaches, rabbits, monastery ruins and recreational facilities. Visitors can sunbathe on the beaches, hire boats and indulge in many sporting activities including canoeing, kayaking, sailing and fishing.

Oslo Opera House is home to the Norwegian National Opera and Ballet, and worth a peek for its bold, new millennium statement to the world. Partly submerged in the sea, this architectural masterpiece rises from the fjord like a massive sheet of ice with angular slabs, similar to giant ski slopes that surprise you at every level. The Opera House design has won many architectural awards.

With so many attractions to see, Oslo makes for a fantastic European destination, both during white snowy winters and long summer days. From medieval architecture to modern day museums, Oslo boasts an abundance of tourist attractions and exciting places of interest that greatly add to its charm and allure.

1. Holmenkollbakken & Skimuseet

In Norway, skiing is more of a religion than a sport, and nothing illustrates this better than the magnificent Holmenkollbakken Ski Jump Tower. As evidenced in ancient cave paintings, Norwegians pretty much inventing skiing, and Holmenkollbakken's museum or Skimuseet, is Oslo's tribute to the sport.

With an elegant curve that reaches for the sky, Holmenkollbakken features a ski jump that towers high above the Oslo cityscape and boasts a reputation as the most modern ski jump in the world. One of the first designer ski jumps created, the Holmenkollen tower comprises an imposing monument of concrete and a hundred tons of steel. In fact, Holmenkollen exists as the world's only steel ski jump.

Situated at Kongeveien, the ski jump was opened officially in 2010 and comprises a start house that rises 60 meters above ground. The ski jump tower was tailor-made for athletes and boasts world-class engineering.

Some of its features include an ice track machine, permanent wind protection, improved snow production facilities, and an upgraded sound and light system. There are also the new Royal grandstand, judge's grandstand and improved facilities for the press and the public.

Visitors can enjoy the thrill of flying 100 meters in the world famous ski jumping hill, inside the ski-simulator. Also located on the grounds is a shop where sleds can be rented per hour or for the day. And if you get too cold you can enjoy a steaming mug of blackcurrant wine or tasty hot chocolate at the café.

For spectacular views of the city and Oslofjord, simply visit the platform at the top of the tower. If you are in the Holmenkollbakken area after dusk, you will enjoy views of the lit up ultra modern ski jump tower that stands out for miles around. You can easily gaze upon it from a distance.

There is also a museum located inside the base of the Holmenkollen Ski Jump Tower. The oldest museum of its kind in the world, the Skimuseet was opened in 1923 and offers information on the history of skiing for the last 4,000 years. It also has an exhibition on snowboarding, in addition to the expeditions of Norwegian polar explorers.

You can also enjoy historic glimpses into the Winter Olympics held in 1994 at Lillehammer and in 1952 in Oslo. Visitors can also view skis from the Viking era, as well as those that belonged to the Norwegian Royal Family.

Holmenkollbakken is a historic landmark in the consciousness of Norwegians which embodies over 100 years of skiing competitions. Ski jumping competitions were already organized in Oslo as early as 1866. In no time, the competition was moved to the hill of Holmenkollen to ensure good snow.

Every winter, Holmenkollen hosts World Cup Nordic skiing events, including Holmenkolldagen, which is like Norway's second National Day. This annual jump competition features thousands of enthusiastic Norwegians and sport lovers, and even the Norwegian Royal Family makes an appearance. There's a great atmosphere to this day, and one that you shouldn't miss out on if you are in Oslo.

No matter what the weather is, spending time at Holmenkollen is always fun. Naturally, winter is Holmenkollen's high season. Popular events and activities held here during this time include ski jumps, slalom, dog sledding, cross-country skiing, winter games for the deaf, in addition to the Holmenkollen Ski Festival.

During the summer, a variety of outdoor recreational activities are held at Holmenkollen. These include cycling, swimming, orienteering, marathons, fishing contests, summer ski jumping, as well as freestyle dog and horse shows. The Summer Concert held in Holmenkollen is also so popular that it is broadcast in other countries.

2. Vikingskipshuset

Norway's rich history of seafaring can be viewed all on display on Oslo's Bygdoy Peninsula, which is home to a number of interesting nautical museums. The most famous of these museums is Vikingskipshuset.

The Vikingskipshuset or Viking Ship Museum in Oslo houses three of the best preserved wooden Viking ships in the world, which were built more than 1200 years ago and discovered over a century ago. Here you can experience the 9th century Viking ships up close and personal, as well as discover more about the way of life – and death – of the Vikings.

Also worth a peek are the small boats, sledges, harnesses and carts with great ornamentation. The ships and artifacts on exhibit at the museum represent the pinnacle of Viking engineering, innovation and skill. The artifacts are primarily from the Oseberg excavation that uncovered the largest collection of Viking age wooden artifacts ever discovered.

At the museum, you can view Norway's largest gold treasure from the Viking era, as well as learn about the life of the Vikings as farmers, warriors and traders by exploring their ornaments, tools, implements, weaponry and household utensils. The museum also features exhibits that demonstrate weaving, textile and fabric techniques of the Viking era.

Another museum on the Bygdoy Peninsula that is worth a visit is Kon-Tiki Museet. Situated close to the Viking Ship Museum, just a short walk away, the Kon-Tiki Museum is home to original artifacts and vessels from world-famous expeditions by Thor Heyerdahl, one of Europe's most famous adventurers, scientists and environmental campaigners of his time.

Thor Heyerdahl gained fame around the world after crossing the Pacific Ocean in 1947 on the Kon-Tiki, sailing by raft from South America to the Tuamotu Islands. He followed this up with other expeditions on the reed boats Ra and Tigris.

Visitors to the museum can enjoy exhibits of the original Kon-Tiki raft, the Fatu-Hiva, the Ra II reed boat, an exhibition on the Tigris, and another on Easter Island which features a 10 meter replica of a statue from Easter Island. There is also a cave tour and an underwater exhibition complete with a life-size whale shark.

The museum also has a souvenir shop and a room for screening films. Here you can learn more about the topographical landscape of Norway by viewing an aerial tour of the Norwegian coastline and settlements.

Once done soaking in the museum exhibits, you can sample the museum's restaurant lunch menu that features authentic Norwegian cuisine, including the Kon-Tiki Fish Casserole and Tapas buffet that come highly recommended. Outside the museum, you can enjoy a wonderful view of the bay from its location close to Oslofjord.

The other museums situated on the Bygdoy Peninsula are the Norwegian Museum of Cultural History, the Fram Museum and the Maritime Museum. Bygdoy Peninsula is itself a one-stop leisure destination situated just west of Oslo's city center. It has beautiful beaches, a number of seafood restaurants and cafés to relax in after an exciting day of museum-hopping.

3. Norsk Folkemuseum

The Norsk Folkemuseum or the "Norwegian Folk Museum" is part of the Norwegian Museum of Cultural History. The open-air museum is situated in Museumsveien, just around the corner from the Vikingskipshuset museum on the Bygdoy peninsula.

Founded in 1894, the museum comprises 160 buildings representing the different Norwegian regions, time periods and differences between social classes, and the country and town. Home to collections from across the nation, the museum exhibits displays on how the Norwegian people lived in Norway from the 1500s to the present day.

The museum collection features over two hundred thousand artifacts including photographs and archivalia within the indoor displays. The artifacts were gathered from all social groups of Norway to provide great insight into the country's different cultures.

Norwegian contemporary history is on display here at Norway's largest museum on cultural history in the form of exhibitions and documentation projects.

Permanent indoor exhibitions include traditional handicraft items, folk costumes, folk art, Sami culture, weapons and toys, as well as pharmaceutical history and other historic artifacts. There is also a range of temporary exhibitions and audience programs held all year round.

During the summer months, different activities are held at the museum on a daily basis. Special program events may include guided tours, baking, and handicraft demonstrations, feeding of animals, as well as horse and carriage rides. The museum also hosts events such as folk dancing, exhibitions, markets and arts and crafts activities.

Upon arrival at the open-air museum, you will be welcomed by a host in traditional folk dress who will guide you through your tour. Visitors will also enjoy a visit to the Gol Stave Church which dates from 1200 and is one of 5 medieval buildings that make up the open-air museum.

4. Den Norske Opera & Ballet

Situated on the bank of Bjorvika district, the Oslo Opera House comprises a distinctive glass and marble building that houses the Norwegian Opera and Ballet. Opened officially in 2008, the Opera House took 5 years to complete and is the largest cultural building to be built in Norway since the beginning of the 14th century.

A work of art in itself, the award-winning Oslo Opera House was named World Cultural Building in 2008. In 2010, the building won the prestigious International Architecture Award, having won the Mies van der Rohe Prize the previous year.

The visually stunning building of the Opera House is located right on the harbor, with an angled white exterior that seems to rise from the water. It is one of the most striking buildings on the city skyline, an iceberg-like structure that impressively rises from the pristine banks of Oslofjord.

From the outside, the building's most striking feature is its white sloping marble roof that rises up directly from the Oslofjord, enabling visitors to enjoy a stroll and take in great views of the city. During the summer, bring your own picnic and eat out on the sloping rooftop while enjoying panoramic views of the city, its fjord and mountains. This location offers one of the best photo ops in the city.

Looking at the Opera House from Oslofjord, you will notice a façade of solar panels. This is in fact the biggest site for solar panels in Norway which supplies the building with some of its energy requirements. The floor area at the base of the building is equivalent to 4 international standard football fields, measuring over 38,000 square meters. The opera house building has 3 stages and over 1000 seats.

The foyer comprises a large open room with minimalist décor, built using simple materials including concrete, stone, wood and glass. Here you will find bars, restaurants and seating areas. Be sure to explore the hushed oak and marble interior where you can have a prawn and egg smorbrod or open sandwich.

The main auditorium takes on the shape of a classic horseshoe reminiscent of classical theatres of bygone eras, and is also one of the world's most technologically advanced. The auditorium design offers great acoustic and fantastic scenographic flexibility. The stage area itself measures several thousand square meters with some parts going as much as 16 meters below the water surface.

In contrast to the light foyer, the main auditorium is decorated in Baltic oak treated with ammonia. On the backs of the 1,350 seats are individual screens with subtitles available in 8 different languages.

The balconies were carved by boat builders from Norway's northwestern coast and hanging from the ceiling is the largest circular chandelier in Norway which measures seven meters in diameter, weighs 8 tons and features over five thousand crystal glass elements.

The rich and varied programs of the Oslo Opera House take place in the Main House which has 1369 seats, the Second House which has 400 seats and the Studio which has 200 seats. The roof and foyer of the Opera House are also used to hold concerts and other cultural events. Large windows positioned at street level provide the public with glimpses of workshop activities and rehearsals.

It is difficult not to be awed by the complexity of this magnificent structure, but a visit here is a must. Performances are held almost every night, with new ballets and operas debuted on a monthly to bi-monthly basis.

Visitors to the Opera House can attend concerts and performances by the Norwegian National Opera & Ballet. The Opera House hosts classics, premiers of new and renowned Norwegian works, in addition to several big concerts and one-off performances.

Radiant with song and music, the opera house is a marble and granite mountain that visitors to Oslo will enjoy seeing and climbing. Although a recent city landmark, the Opera House is already popular with both tourists and locals.

5. Akershus Slott & Festning

Akershus is one of Norway's finest and oldest cultural heritage sites, which houses a diversity of prominent buildings and installations established over a period spanning 700 years. Regarded as a national symbol, Akershus boasts a rich heritage as the seat of government and the heart of many important events over its long history, a legacy that continues to this day.

Situated in the southeastern section of the Oslo city center, Akershus is an important landmark and an integral part of the identity of Oslo. The present city center was established in 1624 beneath the fortifications of Akershus. Forming a distinctive silhouette against the Oslofjord, the fortress grounds and its central location also offer a popular spot of recreation for locals and tourists alike.

Akershus is regarded as a national symbol due to its historic role as the seat for kings and center of government, not to mention the numerous important and dramatic events that have occurred there throughout history. Its national importance lies in the fact that it today serves as the principal venue for state receptions and official functions for the Norwegian government.

The building of the Akershus Castle and Fortress was begun in 1299 under King Haakon V. It was originally built as a royal residence when Oslo first became the Norwegian capital. Completed in the 1300s, the medieval castle offered a strategic location at the very end of the headland, which survived many sieges throughout the ages. The historic interior and stout walls of the complex bear the scars of many battles.

But it was King Christian IV who modernized the castle and had it converted into a Renaissance castle and royal residence during the 17th century, after a fire consumed the entire city. It was later used as a prison, and there is a museum to educate visitors on this particular history of the site. The site is also home to the Royal Mausoleum.

During the 18th century, the fortress was left to fall into decay. But at the end of the 19th century, extensive restoration and renovation projects were carried out on the fortress to refine and highlight its standing as a national monument. Initial work focused on the Middle Ages as a way of bringing to the fore the tangible reminders of Norway's glorious past.

Akershus Festning or the areas surrounding the castle are also a popular venue for holding major events such as concerts, ceremonies and holiday celebrations. During summer, you may witness the Changing of the Royal

Guard. At the Visitor's Centre, you can obtain more information on the history of the castle and fortress, as well as details on upcoming events to be held at the site.

Akershus Fortress makes for a great spot to discover the history of Oslo. There is something at the fortress for all types of history buffs to enjoy. Visitors can explore the beautiful grounds and historic buildings on their own or join a guided tour.

Pay a visit to the Norwegian Resistance Museum, the leading institution on the history of Nazi occupation, which offers exhibitions and library archives, specialist literature and manuscript collections that are open for public viewing.

After a long day of exploring, take a break at Café Festningen or Karpedammen Café, both of which are located on the fortress grounds. Here you can enjoy alfresco refreshments during the summer, whether it's a cup of coffee, a hot meal or some alcoholic beverages.

Karpedammen Café is situated next to the carp pond, within the central fortress area but is closed during inclement weather. The carp pond was recreated in the Sixties, although its origins date back to earlier times as evidenced by maps dating from the end of the 17th century. Café Festningen is located on the lower section of the fortress and serves both hot and cold dishes.

Akershus is well worth a visit for those exploring the beautiful, complex country of Norway, as it takes you on a journey in time, from the 14th century to the present day. For 700 years, the site has been an important part of the culture and history of Oslo. Rich in history, the 13th century attraction is a vibrant presence for Oslo's residents and is easy to access by visitors out exploring the city.

6. Frognerparken

Situated at Kirkeveien/Middelthuns gate, Frognerparken or "Frogner Park" is the largest park in Oslo. A popular spot for recreation among people from around the city, the park gets crowded on warm summer days with many locals who come to enjoy the outdoors, have a barbecue or picnic, play sports, sunbathe or jog.

Located towards Majorstua in one corner of the park is the Frogner Open-Air Bath and Stadium. In the corner by Frogner Plass is the Oslo City Museum and Frogner Manor House. The park also houses the largest collection of roses in Norway, comprising a total of 14,000 plants from 150 diverse species.

However, the most visited park attraction is Vigelandsparken or the Vigeland Sculpture Park which is situated in the middle of Frogner Park. Oslo's famous park, Vigelandsparken is home to 212 bronze, granite and cast iron sculptures of naked men, women and children.

One of the most famous sculptures is *Monolitten* or the Monolith, a spire that rises 17 meters. Carved out of a single piece of white granite, the Monolith comprises 121 commanding human figures. Some of the many interpretations of the Monolith include: the struggle for existence, man's resurrection, man's yearning for spiritual spheres, cyclic repetition and the transcendence of everyday life.

Other famous sculptures include *Sinnataggen* or the Little Angry Boy, along with *Livshjulet* or the Wheel of Life.

Vigeland was a famous Norwegian sculptor who modeled all his sculptures in full size by himself. The bronze casting and stone carvings were completed by other talented craftsmen. Vigeland also designed the layout of the park grounds and architectural setting, including the long straight avenues bordered by maple trees, and the far stretching lawns.

Construction of Vigelandsparken took place over a number of years and the end result produced a monumental artistic creation with a human message that is well worth the visit. The main draw of the life-sized exhibits of Vigelandsparken is that they appear to exude real emotion.

Vigelandsparken constantly hosts hundreds of Norwegians engaged in various leisurely activities, including playing among the famous sculptures. One of Oslo's most beautiful public parks and a popular meeting spot from Oslo's dwellers, the area is also a great place to take a stroll during the winter months.

Visitors can also tour the Vigelandmuseet or "Vigeland Museum" which is situated a five minutes' walk south of the park. The beautiful building that houses the Museum is regarded as one of the finest examples of neo-Classical architecture in Norway.

Step inside and browse the museum collection, which consists of the artist's early works, his monuments, portraits and original full-size plaster models for the sculptures at Vigeland Park. Vigeland's working process has also been well documented in the museum which shows contemporary art exhibits that change regularly.

Inside the Vigeland Museum lies one of Oslo's best kept secrets. Tomba Emmanuelle is the main attraction of the museum, which comprises a dark, barrel-vaulted room that is entirely covered in frescoes. The dark room features an 800 square-meter painting VITA or life, which depicts the dramatic scenes of human life starting from conception to death.

The mausoleum is named after Emanuel Vigeland, brother to Gustav Vigeland who designed the building to serve as his tomb, and whose ashes have been laid to rest inside an urn above the door. Emanuel called the building "Tomba Emmanuelle" in honor of his Italian idols.

Once done exploring the creative worlds of the Vigeland brothers, take a coffee break at Café Vigeland patisserie where you can sink your teeth into French pastries and cakes, baguettes, sandwiches, a variety of coffee and freshly made juice. There is also a gift shop located inside the main entrance to the Sculpture Park, at which you can shop for souvenirs and gift items.

7. Nasjonalgalleriet

Situated at Universitetsgata, Nasjonalgalleriet or the "National Gallery" is home to the largest collection of paintings, sculptures and drawings of Norway. Founded in 1837, the National Gallery is part of Norway's National Museum of Art, Architecture and Design.

The exhibitions found at the gallery present older art, with principal emphasis laid on Norwegian art. There is a permanent exhibition of highlights from the collection, as well as national icons spanning the Romantic period to the mid 20th century. Also on display are the works of international sculptors and painters, including those of the French impressionists.

The main highlights of the museum include *The Scream* and *Madonna* by Edvard Munch, and the paintings of Cezanne and Manet. There are also some fascinating works by Picasso, Van Gogh and Matisse. Also check out Theodor Kittelsens paintings of Norwegian legends such as Nokken, the water spirit, which leave a lasting impression.

Be sure to visit the Fairy Tale Room where you can take a peek at princesses, trolls and other fairy tale creatures from the extensive collections of the museum. In the Drawing Room, visitors can experiment with hard and soft pencils. For inspiration, look at Gustav Vigeland's sculpture

Mother and Child from 1907, which has been positioned in the middle of the room.

8. Det Kongelige Slott & Slottsparken

Det Kongelige Slott is the royal residence of Norway which is located at the top of Karl Johans Gate in Slottsplassen. Although not as well known as the British royalty, Norway does have a royal family and this is where they live. Home to the current monarch King Harald V and Queen Sonja, the Royal Palace is built in neo-Classical style with a façade of stuccoed brick and comprises three floors situated on a hill.

Established in 1825 and completed in 1849, the Royal Palace was built as a royal residence during the reign of King Karl Johan who at the time reigned as king of both Norway and Sweden during the first half of the 19th century. Standing in front of the castle is an equestrian statue of King Karl Johan. During the 90s, the palace was extensively restored and renovated to its former glory by King Harald V.

Although the palace serves as the official residence of the current monarch, it is nevertheless open to the public during summer months. The magnificent building can be viewed only by guided tour where visitors are taken around some of the elaborate state rooms such as the White Parlour, Cabinet Parlour, Mirror Hall, Great Hall, the Palace Chapel, King Haakon VII Suite, and the Family Dining Room.

Surrounding the palace on all sides is the Slottsparken or "Castle Park" which is open to the public and comprises majestic trees, grassy areas, statues and small ponds. Since 1911, there has been a tradition of adding statues and monuments to the park. Among the first were those of Norwegian sculptor Gustav Vigeland and the author, Camilla Collett.

If you tour finds you at the palace around 1.30pm, you'll be in time to watch the Changing of the Guard. When the king is in residence, the Royal Guard band accompanies the change of guard with music.

Karl Johans Gate is itself an attraction. Lying at the heart of Oslo, this is the busiest and best-known thoroughfare in Norway, with tens of thousands of pedestrians using the street on a daily basis. Many important institutions in Norway are located here including the Norwegian Parliament, the National University and the National Theatre. The upper section of the street is used to hold parades.

9. Oslofjord

A cool and contemporary city, Oslo lies at the head of its fjord, which comprises a calm, clear body of water with isolated coves, islets and little pockets of beach.

Oslofjord is a spectacular location to explore, full of historical sites dating from the Middle Ages. The fjord is dotted with numerous tiny islands which are little worlds unto themselves, with their wooden trails, secluded beaches and brightly colored cabins. These islands are great spots to go swimming during the summer when the fjord waters are warm enough to take quick dip.

The islands that make up Oslofjord are incredible examples of Norwegian beauty and nature. Each island has its own unique history, a story to tell and character worth exploring. The Oslofjord islands make for a nice getaway from the hustle and bustle of the city, where you can enjoy some peace and quiet, as well as rest after a day of exploring. So be sure to bring a picnic lunch and blanket with you.

Boats run frequently out to the different islands, including the beautiful Langoyene which is a popular favorite of the summer months. While here, visitors can enjoy the beaches, play sports or simply relax under the Scandinavian sun. You could also visit the ruins of an old cloister and get a glimpse into the history of the island. Langoyene features winding woodland paths, a naturist beach and bar.

Catch a ferry and go island hopping between the islands of the Oslo Fjord. Hovedoya is a popular spot for picnics and sunbathing which houses a 12th century Cistercian monastery built by English monks. On Lindoya, you will find Norwegians tending to their small gardens, while Gressholmen has a nature reserve and café.

10. Munchmuseet

Situated at Toyengata, a short walk from Karl Johan Gate, Munchmuseet houses hundreds of paintings by Norwegian painter, Edvard Munch, who holds a unique position among Nordic painters. Munch Museum is home to the world's largest collection of works by Munch, and offers great insight into the artist's role as a pioneer of expressionism.

The collection comprises of 1,200 paintings, 4,500 drawings, 18,000 prints, 6 sculptures, graphic art and watercolors. The museum also holds some less conventional pieces in Munch's artwork, which include lithographic stones, woodcut plates, etchings, books, newspaper cutouts, and other information that further encapsulates the full career of Norway's adored artist.

The museum is entirely devoted to Norway's most famous artist who painted the renowned *Skrik* (The Scream); and holds two versions of *Skrik*, one each in oil and pastels, with the latter dating from 1910. "The Scream" is an iconic Norwegian painting of existential angst.

The museum collection was left to the city by the artist himself and comprises paintings, drawings and graphical prints. The museum constantly changes the exhibitions to present the variety in Munch's production. There is also a documentary exhibition, in addition to audio tours available in English. Visitors can also browse the souvenir shop for books, shirts, catalogs and posters.

The museum was opened in 1963 in commemoration of what would have been the Norwegian Symbolist painter's 100th birthday.

Copyright 2015. All rights reserved.

Except as permitted under the United States Copyright Act of 1976, reproduction or utilization of this work in any form or by any electronic, mechanical, or other means, now known or hereafter invented, including xerography, photocopying, and recording, and in any information storage and retrieval system, is forbidden without written permission.

The ideas, concepts, and opinions expressed in this book are intended to be used for educational and reference purposes only. Author and publisher claim no responsibility to any person or entity for any liability, loss, or damage caused or alleged to be caused directly or indirectly as a result of the use, application, or interpretation of the material in this book.

Printed in Great Britain
by Amazon.co.uk, Ltd.,
Marston Gate.